Table of Contents

D1241839

FRENCH RIVIERA TRAVEL GUIDE 2023

The Ultimate French Riviera Travel Guide.
Discover Inside Tips, Top Attractions and
Hidden Gems for First Timers.

ANDREW NICHOLAS

Introduction

The French Riviera, also known as the Côte d'Azur, is a stunning stretch of coastline along the southeastern region of France that has been attracting visitors for centuries. With its sparkling azure waters, sun-kissed beaches, and charming towns, the French Riviera is a popular destination for travelers from all over the world. In this travel guide, we'll explore the history of the French Riviera and provide insider tips on the top attractions and hidden gems for first-timers.

My Trip to Nice, French Riviera

My 3-days trip to Nice, French Riviera was one of the most memorable experiences of my life. I had always dreamed of visiting the Côte d'Azur, with its stunning coastline, glamorous towns, and warm Mediterranean climate. Finally, I had the opportunity to make that dream a reality.

I arrived in Nice on a sunny afternoon, feeling both excited and jet-lagged. My hotel was located in the heart of the city, just a few blocks from the famous Promenade des Anglais. After checking in, I decided to take a stroll along the promenade to get a first taste of the French Riviera.

The promenade was everything I had imagined and more. The azure blue sea sparkled in the sun, while palm trees and flower gardens lined the walkway. I watched as people jogged, cycled, and roller-skated along the promenade, enjoying the beautiful scenery.

As the sun began to set, I made my way to a nearby restaurant for dinner. I ordered a glass of local rosé wine and some fresh seafood, including a platter of oysters that were some of the best I had ever tasted. As I savored the flavors, I felt grateful to be in such a beautiful place, enjoying the simple pleasures of life.

The next day, I decided to explore the old town of Nice. I wandered through narrow streets lined with colorful buildings, shops, and cafés. I stumbled upon a bustling food market, where vendors sold everything from fragrant spices to artisanal cheeses. I sampled some of the local specialties, such as socca (a chickpea pancake) and pissaladière (a type of pizza with onions and anchovies).

In the afternoon, I took a bus to the nearby town of Villefranche-sur-Mer. This picturesque town is known for its colorful fishing boats, pastel-colored houses, and stunning views of the sea. I walked along the waterfront, admiring the boats and soaking up the Mediterranean sun.

On the third day, which was my final day in Nice, I decided to take a day trip to Monaco. The principality is just a short train ride away from Nice and is known for its luxurious casinos, yacht-lined harbor, and famous Formula 1 race. I walked around the famous Monte Carlo casino, admiring the glamorous architecture and people-watching.

As I headed back to Nice on the train, I felt grateful for the experience of visiting such a beautiful and unique part of the world. The

French Riviera had exceeded all my
expectations, and I knew I would always
treasure the memories of my trip to Nice
and most definitely be back to explore other
towns on the French Riviera like Antibes,
Saint-Tropez, and Monaco.

About the French Riviera

The French Riviera is located on the
Mediterranean coast of southeastern
France, stretching from Menton near the
Italian border to Saint-Tropez in the west.
It includes the famous cities of Nice,
Cannes, and Monaco, as well as smaller
towns like Antibes, Juan-les-Pins, and
Villefranche-sur-Mer. The region is known
for its glamorous lifestyle, luxurious
resorts, and beautiful beaches, as well as its
rich history and cultural heritage.

History of the French Riviera

The French Riviera has a long and
fascinating history, dating back to ancient
times when it was inhabited by Ligurian
tribes. In the Middle Ages, the region was
ruled by various feudal lords and was often
contested between France and Italy. It
wasn't until the 19th century that the
French Riviera began to gain international
fame as a fashionable resort destination for
the wealthy and famous.

One of the most influential figures in the
history of the French Riviera was Queen
Victoria, who visited the region in 1895 and
helped to popularize it among the British
elite. The region also attracted many artists
and writers, including Pablo Picasso, Henri
Matisse, and F. Scott Fitzgerald, who found

inspiration in its natural beauty and cultural richness.

During World War II, the French Riviera played a significant role in the Allied invasion of France, as it was the site of several key battles and strategic operations. After the war, the region experienced a boom in tourism and became known as a playground for the rich and famous, thanks in part to the Cannes Film Festival, which was first held in 1946.

Today, the French Riviera continues to attract visitors from all over the world, who come to enjoy its stunning scenery, rich cultural heritage, and glamorous lifestyle.

Why Visit the French Riviera

There are many reasons why the French Riviera should be on your travel bucket list. Here are some of the top reasons to visit this beautiful region:

Stunning Scenery: The French Riviera boasts some of the most beautiful landscapes in the world, with turquoise waters, sandy beaches, and dramatic cliffs. There are activities for everyone, whether you want to laze on the beach or discover the region's natural wonders.

Culture and History: The French Riviera has a rich cultural history, with museums, galleries, and historical landmarks to explore. From the medieval village of Eze to the ancient Roman ruins of Fréjus, there's plenty to discover in this region.

Delicious Cuisine: French cuisine is renowned around the world, and the French Riviera is no exception. From fresh seafood to local specialties such as socca and pissaladière, there are plenty of delicious dishes to try.

Luxury Lifestyle: The French Riviera is synonymous with luxury, and visitors can indulge in everything from high-end shopping to glamorous nightlife. Whether you're looking to sip champagne on a yacht or dance the night away in a chic club, the French Riviera has something for everyone.

Outdoor Activities: With its beautiful weather and stunning landscapes, the French Riviera is the perfect destination for outdoor enthusiasts. From hiking and biking to watersports and golfing, there are plenty of activities to keep you busy.

Best Time to Go

The French Riviera is a year-round destination, but the best time to visit depends on your preferences. If you want to enjoy the warm weather and sunbathe on the beaches, the summer months (June to August) are the best time to visit. However, keep in mind that this is the peak tourist season, and prices for accommodation and activities can be significantly higher. Additionally, it can get very crowded during this time. Some of the best places to visit during the summer include: Saint-Tropez, Monaco, Menton, Saint-Jean-Cap-Ferrat.

If you prefer a quieter time to visit, consider going in the shoulder seasons (March to

May or September to November). During this time, the weather is still warm and pleasant, and you can avoid the crowds and high prices. However, keep in mind that some attractions may have shorter opening hours or be closed during this time.

Some of the best places to visit during the spring (March to May) include: Nice, Cannes, Antibes, Saint-Tropez.

Some of the best places to visit during the fall (September to November) include: Eze, Grasse.

If you're interested in winter sports, consider visiting during the winter months (December to February). The French Riviera is home to several ski resorts, such as Isola 2000 and Valberg, which offer skiing, snowboarding, and other winter activities. Some of the best places to visit during the winter include: Grasse, Valberg.

Chapter 1

Planning your Trip

Planning a trip to the French Riviera can be overwhelming, especially if you're a first-timer. In this chapter, we'll cover everything you need to know to plan a perfect trip, including, what to pack, and how to get there.

What to Pack

What to pack for your trip to the French Riviera will depend on the time of year you're visiting and what activities you plan to do. However, here are some essential items to bring:

Sunscreen: The sun can be intense, especially during the summer months. Bring sunscreen with a high SPF and apply it frequently throughout the day.

Swimsuit: If you're planning on hitting the beaches, don't forget your swimsuit.

Comfortable walking shoes: The French Riviera is a beautiful place to explore on foot, so bring comfortable shoes for walking.

Light clothing: During the summer months, it can get very hot, so pack light, breathable clothing.

Layers: Even in the warmer months, the evenings can be cooler, so bring layers for when the temperature drops.

Sunglasses and a hat: Use sunglasses and a hat to shield yourself from the sun.

Travel adapter: The electrical outlets in France are different from those in other countries, so bring a travel adapter if needed.

How to Get There

The French Riviera is well connected to the rest of Europe and the world, with several airports, train stations, and highways.

Flights: The French Riviera is well-connected to major cities in Europe and the world. The main airports serving the French Riviera are Nice Côte d'Azur Airport (NCE) and Cannes-Mandelieu Airport (CEQ). There are several airlines that fly to these airports, including Air

France, British Airways, and Lufthansa. To get to your destination from the airport, take a bus or a taxi.

By Train: The French Riviera is well connected by train, with several high-speed trains running from Paris, Lyon, and Marseille. The main train stations on the French Riviera are Nice-Ville, Cannes, and Antibes.

By Car: If you prefer to drive, the French Riviera is well connected to the rest of France and Europe by highways. However, keep in mind that driving in the French Riviera can be challenging, especially during the peak tourist season when the roads can get congested.

Visa Requirements

Depending on the country you are from and how long you plan to remain, different visas are required. It is not necessary to obtain a visa in order to enter France if you are a citizen of the European Union, Switzerland, Norway, Iceland, or Liechtenstein. A current passport or national ID card is required, though.

It's possible that you require a visa to enter France if you're a citizen of a nation outside the European Union. The website of the French Ministry of Foreign Affairs has information about visa requirements. Additionally, you can apply for a visa at the French embassy or consulate in the nation where you currently reside.

If you are a citizen of a country that is part of the Schengen Agreement, you can enter France with a Schengen visa. The Schengen visa allows you to stay in France and other Schengen countries for up to 90 days within a 180-day period.

You must present the following documentation to apply for a Schengen visa:

- A valid passport or travel document
- A completed visa application form
- Two passport-size photos
- Proof of travel insurance
- Proof of accommodation
- Proof of sufficient funds to cover your stay
- A round-trip flight reservation
- Proof of employment or study

Where to Stay

The French Riviera offers a range of accommodation options, from luxury hotels to budget-friendly hostels. Here are a few popular areas to consider when deciding where to stay:

Nice: Nice is the largest city on the French Riviera and offers a range of accommodation options to suit all budgets. It's a great base for exploring the surrounding areas and has a lively atmosphere.

Cannes: Cannes is a popular destination for its glamorous lifestyle, luxury hotels, and famous film festival. If you're looking for a high-end experience, Cannes is a great choice.

Saint-Tropez: Saint-Tropez is known for its beautiful beaches and luxury yachts. It's a great destination for those looking to soak up the sun and indulge in some upscale shopping.

Antibes: Antibes is a charming town that offers a more laid-back atmosphere than some of the larger cities on the French Riviera. It's a great choice for those looking for a quieter holiday.

Types of Accommodations

The French Riviera offers a range of accommodations, from luxury hotels to budget-friendly hostels. When choosing your accommodation, consider factors such as location, amenities, and budget. It's also important to book your accommodation well in advance, especially if you're traveling during peak season, as the French Riviera can be a popular destination for tourists.

Here are the most common types of accommodations available in the French Riviera:

1. Hotels: The French Riviera is known for its luxury hotels, some of which date back to the 19th century. These hotels offer stunning views of the Mediterranean Sea and are equipped with top-notch amenities such as swimming pools, spas, and fine dining restaurants. But these hotels can be quite pricey, especially in the summer.

2. Apartments: Renting an apartment is a popular option for those who want more space and privacy. Many apartments in the French Riviera come equipped with full kitchens, which can be convenient for families or groups who want to save money by cooking their own meals.

3. Villas: If you're traveling with a large group or want to splurge on a luxurious vacation, renting a villa can be a great option. Villas in the French Riviera are often equipped with private pools, spacious living areas, and stunning views of the sea.

4. Bed and Breakfasts: For a more intimate experience, you may want to consider staying at a bed and breakfast. These accommodations offer a homier atmosphere, with personalized attention from the owners.

5. Hostels: If you're traveling on a budget, hostels can be a great option. The French Riviera has several hostels that offer dorm-style rooms and communal areas for socializing.

6. Campgrounds: For outdoor enthusiasts, camping can be a great way to experience the beauty of the French Riviera. There are several campgrounds located throughout the region, some of which offer stunning views of the sea.

Getting Around

The French Riviera is well connected by public transport, making it easy to explore the area without a car. Here are a few options for getting around:

Train: The train is the easiest and most convenient way to get around the French Riviera. The main train line runs from

Cannes to Ventimiglia in Italy and stops at all the major towns along the coast.

Bus: Buses are a cheaper alternative to the train and also offer access to some of the smaller villages that aren't on the main train line.

Taxi: Taxis are readily available in the larger towns and cities, but they can be expensive.

Car rental: If you're planning on exploring the surrounding areas and villages, renting a car can be a good option. However, be aware that parking can be difficult in some of the busier towns.

Bicycle: The French Riviera is a great place to explore by bike, with many bike paths and rental shops available.

Overall, the French Riviera is a beautiful destination that offers something for everyone. By considering where to stay and how to get around, you can ensure that your trip is as smooth and enjoyable as possible.

Chapter 2

Exploring the French Riviera

1. NICE

Nice is one of the most popular destinations
in the French Riviera, attracting visitors
from all over the world with its stunning
coastline, historic old town, and world-class
museums and galleries. Here are some of
the top things to see and do in Nice:

Old Town: The Old Town of Nice, also
known as Vieux Nice, is a charming and
historic district full of winding cobblestone
streets, colorful buildings, and lively cafes
and restaurants. Visitors can stroll through
the narrow alleys and discover hidden
courtyards, explore the daily market at
Cours Saleya, and admire the Baroque

architecture of the 17th-century Palais
Lascaris. Don't miss the iconic Colline du
Chateau, a hilltop park offering panoramic
views of the city and the Mediterranean
Sea.

Promenade des Anglais: The
Promenade des Anglais is a legendary
seafront promenade that stretches for 7 km
along the Bay of Angels. It's a popular spot
for jogging, cycling, and rollerblading, as
well as for enjoying the sunshine and
people-watching. The promenade is lined
with elegant Belle Epoque buildings, luxury
hotels, and chic cafes, and offers stunning
views of the turquoise sea.

Museums and Art Galleries: Nice has a
rich cultural heritage, and there are
numerous museums and art galleries worth
visiting. The Musée Matisse is dedicated to

the life and work of the famous French painter, while the Musée d'Art Moderne et d'Art Contemporain showcases contemporary art from around the world. The Chagall Museum houses a collection of works by the Russian-French artist Marc Chagall, while the Musée des Beaux-Arts features a wide range of European paintings and sculptures.

Parks and Gardens: Nice is known for its beautiful parks and gardens, which offer a welcome respite from the bustling city streets. The Jardin Albert Ier is a popular spot for picnicking and sunbathing, while the Parc de la Colline du Château offers shady paths, waterfalls, and stunning views. The Promenade du Paillon is a modern park that runs through the heart of the city, featuring fountains, sculptures, and children's play areas.

Day trips from Nice: There are many charming towns and villages within easy reach of Nice, making it an ideal base for day trips. Antibes, just 20 km away, is a picturesque town with a charming old town and a beautiful marina. Cannes, known for its international film festival, is just 30 km away and offers sandy beaches and designer boutiques. For a taste of rural Provence, head to Grasse, 40 km away, known for its perfume industry and stunning hilltop location.

2. CANNES

Cannes, located on the French Riviera, is a luxurious resort town famous for its glitz and glamor. The city is known for hosting the Cannes Film Festival, which attracts celebrities and movie buffs from all around the world. However, there is much more to

Cannes than just the Film Festival. In this chapter, we will explore some of the best things to see and do in Cannes.

The Croisette: The Croisette is Cannes's most famous boulevard. This palm-lined promenade stretches along the city's waterfront, offering stunning views of the Mediterranean Sea. The Croisette is home to some of the most expensive hotels, shops, and restaurants in Cannes. It is a great place for a leisurely stroll, people-watching, and taking in the glamorous atmosphere.

Palais des Festivals et des Congrès: The Palais des Festivals et des Congrès is the venue for the Cannes Film Festival. It is also a conference center that hosts many other events throughout the year. Visitors can take a guided tour of the Palais to learn more about its history and see the grand auditorium, where the film screenings take place.

Museums and Art Galleries: Cannes is home to several museums and art galleries that showcase the city's rich history and cultural heritage. The Musée de la Castre is a medieval castle that houses a collection of art and artifacts from around the world. The Musée de la Mer is a maritime museum that displays a range of marine life and shipwreck artifacts. The Centre d'Art La Malmaison is an art gallery that features contemporary art exhibitions.

Beaches: Cannes has some of the most beautiful beaches on the French Riviera. The most famous of these is Plage de la Croisette, which is located on the Croisette. This beach is popular with tourists and locals alike and offers stunning views of the Mediterranean Sea. Other beaches worth visiting in Cannes include Plage du Midi, Plage de la Bocca, and Plage Gazagnaire.

Day Trips From Cannes: There are several beautiful towns and villages near Cannes that are worth visiting. Antibes, located just 20 minutes away from Cannes, is a charming town with a beautiful old town and a lovely marina. Saint-Paul-de-Vence, a medieval hilltop village, is known for its narrow streets, art galleries, and stunning views of the countryside. The town of Grasse, known as the perfume capital of the world, is located just a short drive from Cannes and is home to several perfume factories and museums.

3. SAINT-TROPEZ

Saint-Tropez is a picturesque town on the French Riviera, known for its luxurious yachts, designer boutiques, and trendy beach clubs. The town has a long history dating back to the 10th century, and has been a popular tourist destination since the 1950s, when it became famous as a playground for the rich and famous.

Old Town: One of the must-see areas in Saint-Tropez is the charming Old Town, also known as La Ponche. This area is a maze of narrow streets and alleys lined with colorful houses, shops, and restaurants. The highlight of the Old Town is the 16th-century Citadelle, a fortress that offers panoramic views of the town and the sea. There are plenty of shops, cafes, and restaurants to explore, as well as a vibrant market on Tuesdays and Saturdays.

Beaches: Saint-Tropez is also famous for its beaches, which are some of the most beautiful in the French Riviera. Some of the most popular ones include Pampelonne Beach, Tahiti Beach, and Plage de la Ponche. These beaches offer crystal-clear waters, soft sand, and stunning views of the Mediterranean Sea. Many of them also have beach clubs and restaurants where you can relax and enjoy a cocktail or a meal.

Museums and Art Galleries: Saint-Tropez is home to several museums and art galleries that are worth a visit. The Musée de l'Annonciade is a museum of modern art located in a former chapel. It features works by some of the most famous artists of the 20th century, including Matisse, Derain, and Bonnard. Another interesting museum is the Musée de la

Gendarmerie et du Cinéma, which showcases the history of the town's police force and its links to the film industry. The Musée des Papillons is another famous museum, featuring a collection of over 35,000 butterflies and moths from around the world.

Day Trips from Saint-Tropez: There are also plenty of day trips you can take from Saint-Tropez to explore the surrounding area. One popular option is to visit the nearby town of Ramatuelle, which is known for its beautiful beaches and charming old town. Another option is to take a boat trip to the nearby islands of Porquerolles or Port-Cros, which offer stunning natural scenery and crystal-clear waters for swimming and snorkeling.

4. ANTIBES AND JUAN-LES-PINS

Antibes and Juan-les-Pins are two neighboring towns on the French Riviera that offer a charming mix of history, culture, and seaside relaxation. Antibes has a rich history that dates back to ancient times and is home to a stunning old town, while Juan-les-Pins is known for its beautiful beaches and vibrant nightlife. Together, they make for an unforgettable vacation destination.

Old Town: Antibes' Old Town is a must-see for anyone visiting the French Riviera. The town's historic ramparts, which were built in the 16th century to protect the town from invasion, are a UNESCO World Heritage Site. Within the walls of the Old Town, you'll find narrow, winding streets lined with colorful buildings, charming boutiques, and excellent restaurants. Take a stroll through the Marché Provençal, a lively open-air market where you can sample local specialties like olives, cheeses, and fresh produce.

Beaches: Juan-les-Pins is famous for its beautiful beaches, and there are plenty to choose from. Plage de la Gravette is a popular spot for families, with calm waters and plenty of amenities like showers and restrooms. Plage de la Salis is another excellent option, with a wide stretch of sand and crystal-clear water. If you're looking for a more secluded beach experience, head to Cap d'Antibes and discover hidden coves and small, quiet beaches.

Picasso Museum: Antibes is home to the Picasso Museum, located in the historic

Château Grimaldi. The museum showcases a collection of over 250 works by the famous artist, including paintings, sculptures, and ceramics. Picasso spent time in Antibes in 1946 and used the Château Grimaldi as his studio during his stay. There is a lovely patio with breathtaking views of the Mediterranean located within the museum as well.

Day Trips: Antibes and Juan-les-Pins are both well-connected to other destinations on the French Riviera, making them an excellent base for day trips. One popular option is to visit Cannes, just a short drive away. Cannes is famous for its film festival and luxury shopping, and you can spend the day exploring the designer boutiques and strolling along the famous Croisette promenade.

Another option is to head inland to Grasse, known as the perfume capital of the world. Grasse is home to several perfumeries, and you can take a tour to learn about the history and process of making perfume. The town's picturesque streets and stunning views of the surrounding countryside make it a lovely day trip destination.

5. MONTE CARLO CASINO

Monaco, a sovereign city-state on the French Riviera, is famous for its luxurious lifestyle, charming streets, and stunning landscapes. From the Monte Carlo Casino to the Prince's Palace of Monaco, there's plenty to see and do in this small yet charming destination.

One of the most iconic landmarks in Monaco is the Monte Carlo Casino.

Established in 1863, this lavish casino features an array of gaming options, including slot machines, roulette, blackjack, and poker. However, the casino is not only about gambling but also its stunning architecture and its surrounding gardens. You can also visit the adjacent Opera de Monte-Carlo, which is equally impressive.

Prince's Palace Of Monaco: Another must-see attraction in Monaco is the Prince's Palace of Monaco, the official residence of the Prince of Monaco. This stunning palace dates back to the 13th century and features a mix of architectural styles, including Renaissance and Baroque. Visitors can take a guided tour of the palace's state apartments, throne room, and even see the changing of the guard ceremony.

Oceanographic Museum: For marine lovers, the Oceanographic Museum, founded by Prince Albert I, is another must-visit destination in Monaco. This museum boasts over 6,000 specimens of marine life, including sharks, sea turtles, and octopuses. The museum also houses the Mediterranean Science Commission, which focuses on studying marine life and habitats in the Mediterranean.

Gardens and Parks: When it comes to outdoor spaces, Monaco doesn't disappoint. The Princess Grace Rose Garden is a beautiful oasis, featuring over 8,000 rose bushes, as well as other plants and flowers. The garden is dedicated to the memory of Princess Grace Kelly, who was a great lover of roses. The Japanese Garden, another beautiful green space, features tranquil ponds, bridges, and winding paths.

Day trips from Monaco: If you're interested in exploring beyond Monaco's borders, there are plenty of fantastic day trips to take. Nice, a vibrant and colorful city on the coast, is just a short train ride away. You can explore its historic Old Town, sample some of its famous cuisine, or take a stroll along the Promenade des Anglais.

Another popular day trip is to the hilltop village of Eze, which offers panoramic views of the Mediterranean. The village's cobblestone streets, charming boutiques, and artisan workshops make for a delightful and immersive experience.

Other places to visit on the French Riviera that are often overlooked by tourists include:

6. MENTON

Located just a few kilometers from the Italian border, Menton is a charming town known for its stunning gardens, colorful buildings, and beautiful beaches. One of the most famous attractions in Menton is the Jardin Serre de la Madone, which is home to an impressive collection of exotic plants and flowers. The old town of Menton is also worth exploring, with its narrow winding streets and pastel-colored buildings. If you're looking to relax on the beach, head to Plage des Sablettes or Plage du Fossan.

7. GRASSE

Grasse is known as the perfume capital of the world, and it's a must-visit destination for anyone interested in fragrances. The town has a long history of perfume production, and visitors can take a tour of one of the many perfume factories and learn about the process of creating fragrances. In addition to perfume, Grasse is also home to some beautiful historic buildings, including the 12th-century Cathedral of Notre-Dame-du-Puy.

8. EZE

Perched on a hill overlooking the Mediterranean Sea, Eze is a picturesque village that's worth a visit for its stunning views alone. The town is also home to the Jardin Exotique d'Eze, a botanical garden that's home to a wide variety of exotic plants and flowers. In addition to the garden, Eze is known for its charming medieval streets, which are lined with artisan shops and restaurants serving up delicious local cuisine.

9. VILLEFRANCHE-SUR-MER

Villefranche-sur-Mer is a beautiful town located just a few kilometers east of Nice. The town is known for its beautiful beaches and picturesque harbor, which is often filled with colorful fishing boats. One of the most popular attractions in Villefranche-sur-Mer is the 16th-century Citadelle Saint-Elme, which offers stunning views of the town and the surrounding coastline.

10. SAINT-JEAN-CAP-FERRAT

Located between Nice and Monaco, Saint-Jean-Cap-Ferrat is a picturesque peninsula that's known for its beautiful villas and gardens. The town is home to several stunning beaches, including the Plage de Passable and Plage de la Paloma. One of the top attractions in Saint-Jean-Cap-Ferrat is the Villa Ephrussi de Rothschild, a beautiful mansion that's home to a museum and stunning gardens.

Overall, the French Riviera is full of beautiful destinations to explore, from charming towns to stunning beaches and gardens. Whether you're looking for relaxation or adventure, there's something for everyone on this beautiful stretch of coastline. Be sure to add these lesser-known destinations to your itinerary for a truly unforgettable trip to the French Riviera.

Chapter 3

Beyond the French Riviera

There are plenty of other beautiful destinations that you can explore during your visit to Southern France. Provence, Corsica, and the Italian Riviera are all worth adding to your itinerary, whether you're looking to experience more of the Mediterranean lifestyle, soak up the local culture, or simply relax and enjoy the scenery. In this chapter, we'll take a closer look at each of these destinations and what they have to offer.

Provence

Southeast France, Provence is a region renowned for its stunning landscapes, quaint towns, and vibrant lavender fields. It is a popular destination for tourists who want to experience the French way of life and enjoy the region's natural beauty. Some of the top attractions in Provence include the Roman ruins in Orange, the Palace of the Popes in Avignon, and the picturesque village of Gordes.

One of the most popular ways to explore Provence is by car, as it allows you to see the region's countryside and visit smaller towns and villages. You can also explore the region by bike, as there are plenty of cycling routes that take you through the countryside and along the coast. If you're a foodie, Provence is also known for its delicious cuisine, including bouillabaisse, ratatouille, and aioli.

Corsica

Corsica is an island located southeast of France in the Mediterranean Sea. It is a popular destination for beach lovers, as it has some of the most beautiful beaches in Europe. Corsica is also known for its rugged landscapes, picturesque villages, and rich history. Some of the top attractions in Corsica include the citadel of Calvi, the Bonifacio cliffs, and the Scandola Nature Reserve.

If you're looking to explore Corsica, one of the best ways to do so is by hiking. There are plenty of hiking trails that take you through the island's rugged landscapes and offer stunning views of the coastline. You can also explore the island by boat, as there are plenty of boat tours that take you along the coast and to some of the more secluded beaches. If you're a foodie, Corsica is known for its delicious charcuterie and cheese.

Italian Riviera

The Italian Riviera is a stretch of coastline in Northern Italy that is known for its picturesque towns, colorful buildings, and beautiful beaches. It is a popular destination for tourists who want to experience the Italian way of life and enjoy the region's natural beauty. Some of the top attractions in the Italian Riviera include the five towns of Cinque Terre, Portofino, and the city of Genoa.

One of the best ways to explore the Italian Riviera is by train, as there is a train line that connects all the major towns and cities along the coast. This allows you to easily visit multiple destinations during your trip. You can also explore the region by boat, as there are plenty of boat tours that take you along the coast and to some of the more secluded beaches. If you're a foodie, the Italian Riviera is known for its delicious seafood, pesto, and focaccia.

While the French Riviera is a beautiful destination in its own right, there is plenty to see and explore beyond its borders. Whether you're looking to experience more of the Mediterranean lifestyle, soak up the local culture, or simply relax and enjoy the scenery, Provence, Corsica, and the Italian Riviera are all worth adding to your itinerary. So, plan your trip accordingly and get ready to embark on an unforgettable adventure!

Chapter 4

Hidden Gems And Off-the-Beaten-path Destinations

If you're planning a trip to the French Riviera, you're probably already aware of the region's most popular destinations such as Nice, Cannes, and Saint-Tropez. While these cities are certainly worth visiting, the French Riviera is also home to many hidden gems and off-the-beaten-path destinations that are equally as beautiful and interesting.

Èze Village

Perched on a rocky hilltop overlooking the Mediterranean, Èze Village is a charming medieval town that's often overlooked by tourists. The village is known for its winding cobblestone streets, ancient stone houses, and stunning views of the sea. Be sure to visit the Jardin Exotique d'Eze, a botanical garden filled with exotic plants and sculptures, and the Château de la Chèvre d'Or, a luxurious hotel and restaurant with panoramic views.

Saint-Jean-Cap-Ferrat

Located between Nice and Monaco, Saint-Jean-Cap-Ferrat is a peaceful and picturesque peninsula that's home to some of the French Riviera's most beautiful villas and gardens. Visit the Villa Ephrussi de Rothschild, a stunning mansion filled with art and antiques, and the Jardin botanique exotique de la Villa Thuret, a botanical garden filled with exotic plants and trees. Don't miss the chance to swim in the clear turquoise waters of Paloma Beach, one of the region's best beaches.

Gourdon

Perched on a hilltop in the hinterland of Nice, Gourdon is a medieval village that's known for its stunning views of the mountains and countryside. Explore the narrow streets lined with artisanal shops and cafés, and visit the Château de Gourdon, a 13th-century fortress that's now a museum. If you're a fan of lavender, be sure to visit the nearby Plateau de Valensole, where you'll find fields of lavender in bloom during the summer months.

Roquebrune-Cap-Martin

Located between Monaco and Menton, Roquebrune-Cap-Martin is a charming medieval village that's perched on a rocky hilltop overlooking the sea. Explore the narrow streets lined with stone houses and shops, and visit the Château-Musée de Roquebrune, a museum housed in a 10th-century castle. Don't miss the chance to take a walk along the Sentier du littoral, a scenic coastal path that offers stunning views of the sea and the coastline.

Les Gorges du Verdon

Located in the Var region of the French Riviera, Les Gorges du Verdon is a spectacular canyon that's often called the "Grand Canyon of Europe." The canyon is over 20 kilometers long and up to 700 meters deep, and it's filled with crystal-clear turquoise water. Take a boat ride or kayak through the canyon to experience its beauty up close, or hike the Sentier Martel, a challenging but rewarding hiking trail that takes you through the heart of the canyon.

Saint-Paul de Vence

This medieval hilltop town is a favorite of artists and writers, who come here for the picturesque cobblestone streets, charming boutiques, and galleries showcasing the works of local artisans.

Villefranche-sur-Mer

This charming fishing village is located just a short train ride from Nice and offers a glimpse into traditional French coastal life. With its colorful houses, beautiful beaches, and scenic harbor, Villefranche-sur-Mer is a wonderful place to relax and soak up the local atmosphere.

Chapter 5

Activities and Attractions

The French Riviera is renowned for its stunning beaches, world-class museums and galleries, and exciting festivals and events. Whether you're looking to relax on the sand, explore the local culture, or immerse yourself in the lively atmosphere, the French Riviera has something for everyone. In this chapter, we'll take a closer look at the top activities and attractions in the region.

Beaches

Some of the most stunning beaches on earth may be found along the French Riviera. Every preference can be satisfied by a beach, which ranges from quiet coves to crowded stretches of sand. The following list includes some of the area's top beaches:

Plage de la Garoupe

This beach, which is in the city of Antibes, is renowned for its pristine seas and breathtaking views of the nearby coastline. Snorkeling and sunbathing are both very popular activities there.

Plage de la Croisette

Over 2 miles of this well-known Cannes beach are dotted with opulent hotels, eateries, and retail establishments. It's a terrific location to take in the glitzy atmosphere and people-watch.

Plage de Pampelonne

Situated near Saint-Tropez, this long, sandy beach is a hotspot for celebrities and jetsetters. It's lined with exclusive beach clubs and restaurants, and the clear water is perfect for swimming and water sports.

Paloma Beach

Nestled in the Cap Ferrat peninsula, this secluded beach is a hidden gem with crystal-clear waters and a peaceful atmosphere.

Museums and Galleries

The French Riviera has a rich cultural heritage, and there are numerous museums and galleries to explore. From contemporary art to ancient history, there's something for every interest. Here are a few of the top cultural attractions in the area:

Musée Matisse

Located in Nice, this museum is dedicated
to the work of the famous French painter
Henri Matisse. It houses a large collection
of his paintings, sculptures, and drawings,
as well as personal objects and
memorabilia.

Musée Picasso

Situated in Antibes, this museum is home
to a significant collection of works by the
Spanish artist Pablo Picasso. The museum
is housed in the former Château Grimaldi, a
medieval castle that offers stunning views
of the Mediterranean.

Villa Ephrussi de Rothschild

This magnificent villa in
Saint-Jean-Cap-Ferrat was built by
Baroness Béatrice Ephrussi de Rothschild
in the early 20th century. It now houses a
museum with an impressive collection of

art and furniture, as well as beautiful gardens with fountains, statues, and exotic plants.

Musée National Marc Chagall

Located in Nice, this museum is dedicated to the works of the famous Russian-French artist Marc Chagall. It's home to a collection of paintings, sculptures, and mosaics

Fondation Maeght

Located in Saint-Paul-de-Vence, this museum houses a stunning collection of modern and contemporary art, set within a beautiful outdoor sculpture garden.

Festivals and Events

The French Riviera is known for its lively atmosphere and exciting festivals and events. From glamorous film festivals to colorful carnivals, there's always something going on. Here are a few of the top events to check out:

Cannes Film Festival

This famous film festival takes place every May in Cannes and attracts celebrities and film industry professionals from around the world. It's a great opportunity to see some of the latest movies and rub shoulders with the stars.

Nice Carnival

This colorful carnival takes place every February in Nice and is one of the largest events of its kind in the world. The carnival features parades, music, and fireworks, and attracts visitors from all over.

Monaco Grand Prix

This iconic Formula One race takes place every May in Monaco and is one of the most prestigious events in the racing calendar. The race takes place on a challenging street circuit through the city, and attracts thousands of visitors each year.

Jazz à Juan

This annual jazz festival, held in Juan-les-Pins in July, features performances by some of the world's top jazz musicians, set against the stunning backdrop of the Mediterranean sea.

Hiking and Outdoor Activities

The French Riviera offers a plethora of outdoor activities for nature enthusiasts. The region has a diverse landscape that includes beautiful beaches, scenic mountain ranges, and breathtaking national parks. Some of the popular outdoor activities to engage in include:

1. Hiking: The French Riviera has several hiking trails that offer spectacular views of the coastline, hills, and mountains. Some of the best hiking trails include the Sentier du Littoral, which is a coastal trail that runs along the Mediterranean Sea, the Massif de l'Esterel, which is a mountain range located between Cannes and Saint-Tropez and the Gorges du Verdon, which is a natural park that features stunning gorges, canyons, and cliffs.

2. Water Sports: If you're a fan of water activities, then the French Riviera has plenty to offer. You can go swimming, snorkeling, scuba diving, kayaking, and paddleboarding in the crystal-clear waters of the Mediterranean Sea. Some of the best spots for water sports are Antibes, Cannes, and Saint-Tropez.

3. Cycling: The region has several cycling trails that are suitable for all levels of cyclists. You can explore the scenic countryside and coastal areas while enjoying the fresh air and beautiful scenery. One of the most famous is the Corniche Road, which winds its way along the coast from Nice to Monaco.

Historical Sites

The French Riviera is steeped in history, with a rich cultural heritage that dates back centuries. From Roman ruins to medieval castles, there are plenty of historical sites to explore.

Palais des Papes: One of the most famous historical sites on the French Riviera is the Palais des Papes in Avignon. This is a UNESCO World Heritage site located in Avignon. It was built in the 14th century and was the residence of the popes during the Catholic Church's Avignon Papacy.

Fort Carré: This is a historic fortress located in Antibes. It was built in the 16th century and played a significant role in the region's defense against pirates and invaders.

Grimaldi Castle: This is a medieval castle located in Cagnes-sur-Mer. It was built in the 14th century and was the residence of the Grimaldi family, who ruled Monaco for several centuries.

Roman Amphitheater: Another must-see historical site is the Roman Amphitheater in Frejus. Built in the 1st century AD, the amphitheater is one of the best-preserved Roman structures in France and is still used for concerts and other events. Other notable historical sites include the medieval village of Eze.

Nightlife and Entertainment

The French Riviera is renowned for its glamorous nightlife and entertainment scene. From chic bars and nightclubs to world-class casinos and cultural events, there's always something happening on the French Riviera after dark.

One of the most famous nightlife destinations on the French Riviera is Saint-Tropez. This glamorous town is home to some of the region's most exclusive clubs and bars, attracting a trendy crowd of jet-setters and celebrities.

Cannes is also known for its vibrant nightlife, with a wide range of bars and clubs to choose from. During the summer months, the town comes alive with the Cannes Film Festival, which attracts the world's top film stars and industry professionals.

Monte Carlo - This is a luxurious destination that features several high-end casinos and clubs that attract the rich and famous from around the world.

For those who prefer a more cultural experience, the French Riviera has plenty to offer. From classical music concerts to art exhibitions, there's something for everyone.

Chapter 6

Shopping

The French Riviera is known not just for its beautiful beaches and charming villages but also for its shopping opportunities. Whether you are looking for locally produced goods or high-end designer items, the French Riviera has something for everyone. In this chapter, we'll explore the best places to shop on the French Riviera, from local markets to designer boutiques and souvenir shops.

Local Markets

If you want to experience the true flavor of the French Riviera, head to one of the local markets. Here, you'll find fresh produce, local handicrafts, and other unique items. The markets are a great place to interact with locals, sample some of the regional specialties, and pick up a few souvenirs. These are some of the best markets to visit:

Marché Forville - This market in Cannes is a foodie's paradise. Here, you'll find everything from fresh seafood to exotic spices and herbs. There are also plenty of vendors selling handmade crafts and souvenirs.

Marché aux Fleurs Cours Saleya - This colorful flower market in Nice is a must-see. In addition to beautiful blooms, you'll find vendors selling artisanal soaps, handmade jewelry, and other unique gifts.

Marché Provençal - This market in Antibes is a great place to pick up locally grown fruits and vegetables, as well as spices, cheeses, and other regional specialties.

Place aux Herbes - Located in the charming town of Vence, this market offers a variety of local produce, flowers, and artisanal products. The market is open every Wednesday and Saturday.

Designer Boutiques

Some of the world's most famous fashion houses have boutiques here, offering the latest in designer clothing, shoes, and accessories. Some of the best designer boutiques on the French Riviera include:

Avenue Montaigne - Located in Cannes, this avenue is home to some of the world's most luxurious fashion brands, including Dior, Chanel, and Louis Vuitton.

- Chanel - This iconic fashion house has a boutique in Cannes, where you can browse the latest collections of clothing, jewelry, and accessories.
- Dior - The Dior boutique in Saint-Tropez is a must-visit for fashionistas. Here, you'll find the latest in haute couture, as well as Dior's signature fragrance and beauty products.
- Louis Vuitton - The Louis Vuitton boutique in Monaco is a shopper's paradise. Here, you'll find luxury handbags, luggage, and other accessories, as well as limited edition collections and one-of-a-kind pieces.

Rue d'Antibes - Located in Cannes, this street is known for its high-end fashion boutiques, including Prada, Gucci, and Hermès.

Promenade des Anglais - Located in Nice, this boulevard offers a variety of designer shops, including Yves Saint Laurent and Givenchy.

Souvenir Shops

No trip to the French Riviera is complete without picking up a few souvenirs. Whether you're looking for something to remember your trip by or a gift for someone back home, there are plenty of souvenir shops to choose from. Some of the best souvenir shops on the French Riviera include:

La Cure Gourmande - This confectionery shop in Nice is a great place to pick up some sweet treats to take home. They offer a range of candies, chocolates, and other confections, all beautifully packaged.

Souvenir d'Antibes - Located in Antibes, this shop offers a variety of souvenirs, including Provencal ceramics, postcards, and local artisanal products.

Fragonard - This perfumery in Grasse is a great place to pick up some of the region's famous fragrances. They offer a range of scents, from floral to spicy, as well as soaps, lotions, and other beauty products.

La Maison de la Lavande - This shop in Eze specializes in lavender products, from scented sachets to soaps and lotions. It's the perfect place to pick up a gift for someone who loves all things lavender.

Tips for Shopping in the French Riviera:
- Always carry cash with you, as some local markets and small shops may not accept credit cards.
- Bargaining is not common in designer boutiques, but it is acceptable in local markets and flea markets.
- Be mindful of pickpockets in crowded areas and keep your valuables close to you.
- Check the opening hours of the shops and markets before you go, as many close in the afternoon for a siesta.

Chapter 7

Food And Drink

The French Riviera is known for its exquisite cuisine and dining culture. With a diverse range of regional specialties and fresh ingredients, the local cuisine is a must-try for any traveler visiting the region. In this chapter, we will explore the local cuisine, top restaurants, and cafes to help you discover the best dining experiences in the French Riviera.

Local Cuisine

The cuisine of the French Riviera is heavily influenced by the Mediterranean and Provencal region. The use of fresh herbs, olive oil, and seafood are the defining features of the local cuisine. Some of the most popular regional dishes include:

1. Socca - a savory crepe made from chickpea flour, olive oil, and salt. This dish is a popular street food in Nice and is usually served hot with a sprinkling of black pepper.

2. Ratatouille - a vegetable stew made with tomatoes, eggplant, zucchini, bell peppers, onions, and garlic. This dish is a staple in Provencal cuisine and is often served as a side dish or main course.

3. Bouillabaisse - a fish stew made with a variety of fish, shellfish, vegetables, and herbs. This dish is a specialty of the port city of Marseille and is typically served with a side of rouille, a garlic mayonnaise.

4. Salade Nicoise - a salad made with lettuce, tomatoes, hard-boiled eggs, olives, anchovies, and tuna. This dish originated in Nice and is a popular lunch option in the region.

5. Pissaladière - a pizza-like dish made with caramelized onions, anchovies, and olives, is another tasty local specialty.

6. Tarte Tropezienne - a sweet brioche filled with cream, is a regional favorite, as is the classic French dessert, crème brûlée.

7. Fougasse - For something a little more unusual, try fougasse, a sweet or savory bread that's similar to focaccia.

Restaurants and Cafes

The French Riviera is home to some of the finest restaurants in the world. From Michelin-starred establishments to casual cafes, there is no shortage of dining options in the region. Here are some of the top restaurants and cafes to try:

La Colombe d'Or
Located in the hilltop village of Saint-Paul-de-Vence, this restaurant has been a favorite among artists and celebrities for over 80 years. A focus on local, fresh ingredients is evident in the menu's classic French cuisine.

Le Louis XV
Located inside the Hotel de Paris in Monte-Carlo, this three-Michelin-starred restaurant is known for its luxurious

atmosphere and impeccable service. The
menu features contemporary French
cuisine with a focus on seafood.

Chez Palmyre

Located in the old town of Nice, this
restaurant has been serving traditional
Niçois cuisine since 1926. The menu
features dishes such as stuffed vegetables,
beef stew, and homemade pasta.

Café de Paris

Located in the heart of Monte-Carlo, this
iconic cafe is known for its outdoor terrace
and lively atmosphere. A focus on steak
frites and escargot ingredients is evident in
the menu's classic French cuisine.

La Petite Maison

Located in the port of Nice, this restaurant
is known for its Mediterranean-inspired

cuisine and lively atmosphere. The menu features dishes such as grilled fish, lamb chops, and pasta with truffles.

In addition to these top restaurants, there are also countless cafes and bistros throughout the region. These cafes are perfect for a quick coffee or light lunch. Some of the top cafes to try include **Cafe de la Place in Antibes, Cafe Florian in Cannes, and Cafe Turin in Nice.**

Wine and Vineyards

The French Riviera is home to some of the most famous wine regions in the world, including Provence and the Côte d'Azur. These areas are known for their warm Mediterranean climate and unique soil composition, which create ideal conditions for growing grapes. As a result, the region produces a variety of high-quality wines, including rosé, red, and white.

One of the best ways to experience the wines of the French Riviera is to visit one of the many vineyards in the region. There are numerous wineries that offer tours and tastings, giving you the opportunity to learn about the wine-making process and sample some of the local varietals. Some of the top vineyards in the area include:

Chateau de Bellet: Located in Nice, this winery has been producing wine since the 17th century. They specialize in red, white, and rosé wines, and offer tours and tastings by appointment.

Chateau Sainte Roseline: This vineyard in Les Arcs produces award-winning rosé wines. They offer tours and tastings daily, as well as a gourmet restaurant.

Domaine de la Croix: Situated in the Var region, this winery produces both red and white wines. They offer tours and tastings by appointment, and also have a restaurant on-site.

Markets and Food Tours

If you're looking for a more immersive food experience on the French Riviera, consider visiting one of the many markets or taking a food tour. These options allow you to taste local specialties and interact with the people who produce them.

Some of the top markets in the area include the Marché Forville in Cannes, the Cours Saleya in Nice, and the Place des Lices in

Saint-Tropez. These markets offer a wide range of local produce, including fresh fruits and vegetables, cheese, bread, and seafood.

If you're interested in a more structured food experience, there are also plenty of food tours available. These tours take you to some of the top foodie destinations in the region, and typically include tastings, demonstrations, and behind-the-scenes access. Some popular food tours on the French Riviera include:

The Nice Food Tour: This tour takes you through the streets of Old Nice, stopping at local food shops and restaurants along the way.

The Cannes Food Tour: This tour explores the culinary scene in Cannes, including a visit to the Marché Forville.

The Antibes Food Tour: This tour takes you through the historic streets of Antibes, with stops at local food shops and a visit to the Picasso Museum.

Côte d'Azur Gourmet Tour: This tour takes you on a journey through the region's culinary landscape, stopping at some of the best restaurants, markets, and food shops along the way. Here, you'll get to taste a variety of local specialties, while learning about the history and culture of French cuisine.

No matter what your food preferences are, the French Riviera has something to offer. From world-class wines to fresh local produce, this region is a food lover's paradise. So be sure to explore the markets, vineyards, and food tours on your next trip to the French Riviera.

Chapter 8

Practical Information

Language and Currency

The official language spoken in the French Riviera is French, but you will find that English is also widely spoken, particularly in tourist areas. However, it is always helpful to learn a few basic French phrases to help you get by. Additionally, it is essential to carry a French phrasebook or a translation app with you in case of language barriers.

The official currency of the French Riviera is the Euro (€). It is advisable to exchange your currency before your trip to avoid any currency exchange fees at the airport. ATMs are readily available throughout the region, and most shops and restaurants accept credit cards.

Learn some basic French phrases

This will help you communicate with locals and show that you respect their language and culture. Simple phrases like

- Bonjour (bohn-zhoor) - Hello/good morning/good afternoon
- Au revoir (oh ruh-vwahr) - Goodbye
- Merci (mehr-see) - Thank you
- S'il vous plaît (seel voo play) - Please
- Comment ça va? (kom-mohn sah vah) - (How are you?)
- Ça va bien, merci (I'm fine, thank you)
- Je ne parle pas français (zhuh nuh parl pah frahn-say) - I don't speak French.

- Parlez-vous anglais ? - Do you speak English?
- De rien (You're welcome)
- Excusez-moi: Excuse me
- Pardon: Sorry
- Bonne journée (bohn jurn-ay) - Have a nice day!

Customs and Etiquette

French culture places significant emphasis on manners and etiquette. Here are some customs and etiquette tips to keep in mind during your visit to the French Riviera:

Greetings: French people usually greet each other with a handshake or a kiss on each cheek.When greeting someone, it is customary to say "bonjour" (hello) or "bonsoir" (good evening) depending on the time of day. If you are entering a shop or restaurant, it is also polite to say "bonjour" to the staff. When meeting someone new, it is essential to use the appropriate title, such as Monsieur (Mr.), Madame (Mrs.), or Mademoiselle (Miss).

Dress Code: The French Riviera is known for its glamorous and fashionable atmosphere, so it's always a good idea to dress nicely when going out. Avoid wearing beachwear or overly casual clothing in public places, especially in upscale areas like Cannes or Monaco. It is advisable to pack smart casual outfits, comfortable shoes, and a light jacket for the cooler evenings.

Tipping: Tipping is not mandatory in France, as service charges are usually included in the bill. However, it is customary to round up the bill or leave a small tip of 5-10% for exceptional service.

Dining Etiquette: French people take their dining seriously and consider it an art form. When dining out, it is customary to wait for the host to begin eating before starting your meal. Additionally, it is essential to use proper cutlery and to keep your hands on the table at all times.

Personal Space: French people value their personal space and may find it uncomfortable if you stand too close or invade their personal space. It is essential to maintain a respectful distance, especially when in crowded areas.

Smoking: Smoking is prohibited in public places, including restaurants, cafes, and bars. However, smoking is allowed in designated smoking areas.

Beach Etiquette: If you are visiting the beaches in the French Riviera, be aware that topless sunbathing is common, but nudity is not allowed. It's also important to respect the privacy of others and not to play loud music or engage in disruptive behavior.

Health and Safety

The French Riviera is generally a safe place to visit, with a low level of crime compared to other European destinations. However, it's always a good idea to take basic safety precautions when traveling anywhere. Keep this in mind:

1. Keep your valuables safe: Like in any popular tourist destination, pickpocketing can be a problem on the French Riviera. Be sure to keep your valuables close to you at all times, and don't leave anything of value unattended.

2. Stay aware of your surroundings: While the French Riviera is generally safe, it's always a good idea to be aware of your surroundings. Stay alert when walking around crowded areas, and avoid any areas that feel unsafe.

3. Be careful on the roads: If you're planning on renting a car or driving while in the French Riviera, be aware that the roads can be narrow and winding in some areas. Take your time and be extra cautious when driving, especially if you're not used to driving on the right side of the road.

4. Watch out for the sun: The French Riviera is known for its sunny weather, but it's important to protect yourself from the sun's harmful rays. Wear sunscreen, a hat, and sunglasses.

5. Stay hydrated: The French Riviera can get hot and sunny, so make sure to drink plenty of water to stay hydrated.

6. Stay safe in the water: If you plan on swimming or participating in water activities, be aware of strong currents and follow all safety guidelines.

7. Be prepared for emergencies: Make sure you have travel insurance that covers medical emergencies and keep emergency numbers handy in case of an accident or other emergency.

8. Stay up to date on travel advisories: Finally, be sure to check for any travel advisories or warnings before you leave for your trip. The U.S. State Department and other government agencies provide up-to-date information on potential risks and dangers in different destinations.

Internet and Communications

Staying connected while traveling is easier than ever, thanks to the widespread availability of Wi-Fi and cellular networks. Here are some tips to help you stay connected while in the French Riviera:

Use Wi-Fi hotspots: Many hotels, restaurants, and cafes in the French Riviera offer free Wi-Fi to their customers. Take advantage of these hotspots to stay connected without using up your data plan.

Get a local SIM card: If you'll be in the French Riviera for an extended period of time, or if you'll need to make a lot of calls or use a lot of data, consider getting a local SIM card for your phone. This will allow you to use local cellular networks at a lower cost than roaming on your home network.

Use messaging apps: Messaging apps like WhatsApp, Viber, and Telegram allow you to make calls and send messages over the internet, rather than using cellular networks. This can be a cost-effective way to stay in touch with friends and family back home.

Be aware of data roaming charges: If you're not using a local SIM card, be aware that data roaming charges can be very expensive. Check with your provider before you leave to see if they offer any international data plans or packages.

Consider a portable Wi-Fi device: If you'll be traveling with a group or need to stay connected on multiple devices, consider renting a portable Wi-Fi device. These devices allow you to connect multiple devices to a single Wi-Fi network, and can be a convenient option if you'll be spending a lot of time on the go.

Conclusion

The French Riviera is a stunning destination that offers visitors a combination of breathtaking natural beauty, rich history, and a vibrant culture. From the glamorous beaches of Cannes and St. Tropez to the charming hilltop villages of Eze and St. Paul de Vence, there is something for everyone on the French Riviera.

If you're planning a trip to the French Riviera in 2023, be sure to use this ultimate travel guide to discover all the top attractions, insider tips, and hidden gems that the region has to offer. Whether you're a first-time visitor or a seasoned traveler, there is always something new to explore and discover on the French Riviera.

One of the key takeaways from this travel guide is the importance of planning ahead and doing your research before you arrive. With so many incredible sights and experiences to choose from, it can be overwhelming to decide what to see and do. By using this guide as a starting point, you can create a customized itinerary that suits your interests, budget, and schedule.

Another important tip is to be open to new experiences and take the time to immerse yourself in the local culture. From sampling delicious Provençal cuisine to attending a traditional French market, there are plenty of opportunities to connect with the people and traditions of the region.

Ultimately, the French Riviera is a place of incredible beauty and endless possibilities.

Whether you're looking for a luxurious beach vacation, a cultural escape, or a scenic road trip, this destination has it all. By following the advice in this travel guide and keeping an open mind, you're sure to have an unforgettable adventure on the French Riviera in 2023.

Encouragement Quotes

Finally, we want to leave you with some encouragement quotes to inspire you on your travels:

The world is a book, and you only read a page when you do not travel - Saint Augustine

"Exploration pays off." - Aesop

The journey, not the destination, is important. - T.S. Eliot

Travel extensively, frequently, and wholeheartedly. : - Unknown

Traveling "leaves you speechless and then turns you into a storyteller," according to one traveler. - A Ibn Battuta

You can only purchase travel to increase your wealth. — Anonymous

Prejudice, intolerance, and narrow-mindedness die when they are exposed to travel - Mark Twain

Useful Websites and Resources

- Official French Riviera Tourism Board Website: https://www.frenchriviera-tourism.com/

- Visit Provence:
  https://www.visitprovence.com/en
- Lonely Planet French Riviera Travel
  Guide:
  https://www.lonelyplanet.com/franc
  e/provence/french-riviera
- Rick Steves' France Travel Guide:
  https://www.ricksteves.com/europe/
  france
- TripAdvisor French Riviera Travel
  Forum:
  https://www.tripadvisor.com/ShowF
  orum-g187216-i137-French_Riviera_
  Cote_d_Azur_Provence_Alpes_Cote
  _d_Azur.html

We hope that this travel guide has been
helpful in planning your trip to the French
Riviera and that you have a wonderful time
exploring this beautiful region. Bon voyage!

Made in United States
North Haven, CT
10 June 2023

37604798R00065